The Seven Critical Website Mistakes

Website Mistakes People Unwittingly
Make, and How To Solve Them

Alun Richards

www.90daybooks.com

First published in Great Britain in 2012 by 90-Day Books, a trading name of Meaningful Goals Ltd., Sussex, England.
www.90daybooks.com

Author's photograph by Maricarmen Forster,
maricarmen@dial.pipex.com
Book design and layout by Kevin Bermingham, 90-Day Books.
Cover design and layout by Kevin Bermingham, 90-Day Books.

British Library Cataloguing in Publication Data.
A catalogue record for this book is available from the British Library.

V2-Pocket edition
ISBN 978-1-908101-14-3

1. Computers & Internet

To Maricarmen, my lovely wife.

Acknowledgements

Maricarmen for her unstinting love, support, friendship, help and for putting up with me for so many years.

Alex Mandossian for his inspirational training in internet marketing, product creation, productivity, running teleseminars and website creation.

Robert Cialdini for his seminal work on social influence.

Russell Brunson for his insights about squeeze pages and product creation.

Armand Morin for his training in internet marketing and website design.

Jason Fladlien for his training and internet marketing products.

Michael Breen for his awesome NLP training and content that I use daily.

Alasdair McWilliam for his friendship, support and source of inspirational ideas.

George Kedourie for his help, friendship, insight and web design ideas that I've found closely parallel mine.

Tim Kenning for his insights into product creation, NLP and more.

Kevin Bermingham, of 90-Day Books, for mentoring me through the book creation and publishing process. I literally couldn't have created this book without him.

All my clients of my website services, my products and my courses. Thank you all!

Also by

Alun Richards

Fire Your Webmaster!

Create Your Own WordPress Website
And Save Yourself A Fortune

Note

Chapter One of '*Fire Your Webmaster!*'

now includes the whole of

'*The Seven Critical Website Mistakes*'

Contents

Why Understand the Critical Problems?

In my many years of creating websites for clients, I have seen a number of problems that come up again and again. They are the problems that have the biggest negative impact on people. They are the fundamental problems that you need to get resolved to build a website that works for you. Any one of these problems can frustrate your chances of being successful online. If you avoid them in the first place, you have a much better chance of succeeding with your website. Let's explore them one by one.

1. Website Not Oriented to Your Market
2. Having a Brochure Website
3. Wrong Hosting
4. Choosing The Wrong Registrar
5. Wrong Domain Name
6. Wrong Technology Choices
7. Poor Look and Feel

The Seven Critical Website Mistakes

1. Website Not Oriented to Your Market

Let's start with the biggest problem of all - a website not oriented to your target market. With some of the website problems I'm discussing, we can change an aspect of the technology used, or a service supplier and resolve the problem.

Not so with this problem. If your website is not oriented to your target market, it's best to take a deep breath, accept the fact and begin planning a website that does appeal to your market.

The sad fact is that if you try to appeal to everyone you will appeal to no-one. Appealing to no-one means you get no site visitors. And this means no list sign-ups and no eyeballs to see the products and services you offer.

So it pays to get clear from the start what it is you offer, and to whom, and to orient your website around that.

What is Your Niche?

In order to be successful in business – any business – you must be crystal clear about exactly who your market niche is.

And your website must reflect this.

It must provide information that your target market want. It must use their unique language. They must feel that it's written for them, or they will go elsewhere.

Your website must be oriented to your target market.

The risk is that if it's not specifically oriented to your target market, your website won't appeal to anyone.

What does Your Market Want?

Your website must offer what your target market uniquely want.

If you know your target market well, you must be aware of their top 3-5 problems. Every market has a set of problems that the members of the market come across again and again.

In recognising what these are, not only do you gain credibility in that market, but you develop rapport with its members instantly.

How do You Know What Your Market Want?

You know what your market want by asking them! More about this later, but there are several effective online means to get information from your market, as well as the more traditional offline ways of getting information.

If you're not sure what your market wants, then the first step is to find out. This will save you perhaps weeks of lost time in developing the wrong product, supplying it via the wrong media or offering it at the wrong price.

Does Your Website Deliver It?

Finally, you must ask yourself whether your website delivers what your target market wants. Not what they need – what they want.

Need and want are two fundamentally different things. You may know precisely what your market need, but there's no point in offering it if they do not want it.

So does your website offer what your target market actually wants, in the format they want, at a price that they can afford?

If you offer solutions to your market's key problems, then you will be a person much in demand. If you don't, your website may need some changes.

2. Having a Brochure Website

What is a brochure website and why should you care?

Definition of a Brochure Site

A brochure site looks just like an online brochure. Often it can look great — typically with well-taken pictures, but with a brochure site there is no interaction with your prospect.

Problems with a Brochure Site

Although it can place you in a good light, a brochure site's lack of interaction with your prospects means that it does not collect leads and it does not sell your offerings.

These are the fundamentals of business –
attracting prospects and converting them
to paying customers.

It's been possible to do both of these
online for years now, and there is no
earthly reason why your website should
not do both.

Does not take leads

What do I mean by not taking leads?

A lead is a prospect who may want to do
business with you. They haven't done
business with you yet, but they are part of
your target market, you know what their
biggest problems are, and you have a
solution that you can sell to them.

The most common way to collect leads is
to capture your prospect's name and
email address via a form on your site.

Once you capture a prospect's details, they are stored securely in an online database. These databases have mechanisms to send emails to your collection of leads, to build the relationship with them, and to make offers to them.

You've probably seen an email capture form on several websites, and have probably signed up to several people's online databases.

It's now straightforward for your website to interact with prospects in this way. You need to have an account with an autoresponder.

E.g. Aweber
http://alunrecommends.com/aweber or
http://1clickshoppingcart.com

The building and maintenance of your online database of prospects is a vital part of your business and we'll return to this several times in this book.

Does Not Sell Your Offerings

The second critical function that your website must perform is it must sell your products or services.

I've mentioned that in having a target market, you must understand the biggest problems experienced by that market.

If you're then able to offer your solutions to those problems at an attractive cost from your website, then you have the basis of a business.

Offering products

Any number of products can be offered from your website. These can range from entry-level products right up to tailored courses.

- PDF tips booklets
- Downloadable eBooks
- Books
- CDs
- DVDs
- Home study courses
- Teleseminar or webinar courses
- Physical seminars and workshops
- Mentoring programmes

All of these products and more can be offered from your website. You can take your customer's payment online via credit card or debit card and ensure that either downloads or physical products are supplied to your new customer.

Offering Services From Your Website

Selling services from your website is similar to selling products. But it's not enough to just passively post a contact number for people to book your services. This simply does not engage people sufficiently.

Intangibility of a service

With a service, there's nothing to see or feel – there's nothing that the prospect can see, that they are going to get. This lack of physical evidence can dissuade people from buying a service from you – they simply don't have any proof of the existence of your service. You therefore must make an intangible service more tangible and real to your prospects.

Here's how you can make an intangible service more tangible.

- Provision of a supporting physical product
- Provision of information
- An opportunity to interact
- A description of your service

So ask yourself, what could I provide to make my service appear more tangible? These days it's possible to add value to a service easily at little cost.

Here are some ideas:

- Downloadable plan that the customer can use.
- A physical workbook that's sent out to them.
- A PDF with instructions for preparing for your service.

- A survey about their possible problems and suggested solutions.
- An audio where you explain the first few steps of your programme.
- A pre-recorded teleseminar or webinar.
- An online video with pre-service exercises.
- An image of your service in a box

Any and all of these strategies can be used to make your service more tangible. The more costly your service, the more of these you want to use.

So what could you offer?

3. Wrong Hosting

Let's start with what hosting is. Hosting is where your website lives. Think of it as a housing estate. Just as houses live on estates, your website lives on hosting. You cannot have a website without hosting.

Hosting (which may also be referred to as web hosting or website hosting) is provided by a hosting company who are responsible for managing the files that make up your website, and who provide a mechanism for them to be visible on the internet. They also provide mechanisms for you to update, delete and backup your website.

You pay a hosting company for an amount of disk space where your website will live and be served up online. You lease both hard disk space and bandwidth from the hosting company, bought via a hosting package that is paid for monthly or yearly. Bandwidth is the amount of data that you're allowed to transfer to and from your website in a month.

Hosting Requirements

You want hosting that meets your needs, and there are certain things you must ensure you get with your hosting. This applies whether you buy your own hosting, or whether it's provided for you in a package, perhaps by your webmaster.

The question to ask is, "Does it give you tools that make the installation of your site quick and easy?"

Getting the Right Hosting

When you buy hosting, there are several things you want to look for.

- Must support WordPress
- Owning your username and passwords
- Multi-domain hosting
- Technology
- Support and Reliability

Must Support WordPress

WordPress is the most used and most trusted way of developing websites. There are many reasons to use WordPress, which we discuss elsewhere. But you want your hosting to support WordPress.

Owning your usernames and passwords

People get into trouble with this time and time again. As your hosting determines whether your website is visible or not, you must have control of your hosting.

This means having the username and password to the control panel AND the username and password for ftp access. Let's explain what those terms mean.

A control panel is a piece of software that allows you to create files, delete them and move them. It also allows you access to your email server configuration. If you don't have this username and password, and someone else does, you are not in control of your website.

Ftp stands for File Transfer Protocol, and is a standard way to upload files to your hosting and to download them to your PC. It also allows deletion and renaming of files. Needless to say, you must be in possession of your ftp username and password, or you lose the ability to control your files.

The importance of this cannot be overstated. It's like designing your dream house and then rather than looking after the keys yourself, you give them to someone else. You wouldn't dream of doing this with your house, but incredibly, people do it with websites all the time.

Always insist on your hosting's control panel username and password and its ftp username and password.

Multi-domain Hosting

A moment ago, we likened hosting to a housing estate. If the estate is your hosting, your house is your website. Most decent estates have more than one house, and that's what multi-domain hosting gives you – the ability to add additional websites as and when you need, without acquiring an entire new estate every time.

If you have the more limited single-domain hosting, you can only host one website on your hosting. This means you need to pay for more hosting every time you need a new website.

With multi-domain hosting, you can host as many websites as you like – within the limits of your allowances. And as multi-domain hosting is only a little more expensive than single-domain hosting, it makes economic sense to get multi-domain hosting from the start.

The Right Technology Environment

Your hosting must support the type of site that you need. Otherwise, you've just wasted your money on hosting.

With more than 71 million users worldwide, I recommend WordPress as the platform for your website.

Your hosting must therefore support WordPress, and facilitate the easy installation and maintenance of WordPress sites.

To run and maintain WordPress, your hosting needs to have a particular environment and it must provide certain functions. If you're unclear whether your hosting is suitable, to run WordPress, it needs the following characteristics:

- Servers based on Linux, not Microsoft
- Fantastastico, that you require to support WordPress

Support and Reliability

Does your hosting supplier offer 24x7 support, or is support only available Monday-Friday 9-5pm? Does your hosting have sufficient technical support people that you can contact? Or is the support simply a list of frequently asked questions?

Reliability

Have a look at the uptime that your hosting provider promises. You want your site to have little or no downtime.

Big enough to be around in five years

Is the hosting provider large enough so that it's likely they will be around in five years?

The last thing you want is to buy hosting, then have to set up somewhere else because your supplier has gone bust.

No Cpanel

Hosting companies need to offer an easy way for you to install applications, set up your email, and another website and to maintain your site.

The most recognised and standard way to do this is to use cpanel.

Cpanel is an industry-standard control panel for managing your hosting. As it's a standard, you'll find a lot of people know how to use it – useful if you get stuck. Also, training in cpanel use is widely available for little outlay – in fact, you may even find your hosting company provides videos on how to use cpanel.

A Hosting Shortcut

Rather than spend time detailing why these characteristics are required, you could either use them as a checklist, or better still, use the hosting that I recommend, and use for myself and my clients, which is the 'Baby' hosting package from http://1clickhostgator.com.

This hosting package has all the requirements I have mentioned, and has all you require to support WordPress effectively and most common functions of cpanel.

4. Choosing The Wrong Registrar

A registrar is the organisation that supplies you with a domain name.

Why Do I Need To Use a Registrar?

In order for your website to operate, it needs a domain name – like Google.com or Amazon.co.uk. This is what you type into your browser window (Internet Explorer, Firefox or Chrome) to get your browser to display your website.

It's a bit like the name of your house, but instead of Dunroamin' it's in at least two parts. You have the top-level domain, like com, co.uk, org or net. And to the left of that, separated by a full stop, is a hopefully memorable name that's chosen by you.

The full domain name might be yourdomain.com.

You need a registrar to supply you with a domain name – one that hasn't already been allocated.

What is a Registrar?

A registrar is an organisation that registers a domain for you and provides you with domain-associated services.

These include services that allow you to see if the domain name you've chosen is available and to point your domain name at the hosting associated with your website.

Typically, a registrar leases the domain name to you for one or more years.

Registrar Problems

Just as you can have problems with hosting, you can have many problems associated with your choice of registrar. Here are some that I've come across.

No Online Control Panel

Usually the way you configure a domain name is via your registrar's control panel. However, a registrar may not have an online control panel that is accessible for its customers. If there is no control panel, the only way you can configure your domain is by requesting those changes by phone or letter.

9-5 Weekday Access

The problem of not having a control panel is compounded if there is poor support, for example if the registrar only answers their phones 9-5pm Monday to Friday.

If you need to change a client's domain outside these hours, you simply have to wait until the office is staffed.

Domain Tied to Hosting

Many hosting companies also have a registrar operation, so you can register domain names as well as purchase hosting. Some small hosting companies sell domain names that cannot be either transferred to other registrars or worse, cannot be re-pointed to other hosting.

What You Need From a Registrar

Here's a shortlist of what to look for in a professional registrar.

- Online Control Panel
- Ease of Use
- Affordability
- Stability - Will Be There in Two Years
- Good Support

Online Control Panel

Your registrar needs an online control panel that allows you to configure your domain name that is available 24 hours a day, 7 days a week. You should be able to buy domains online quickly and easily, preferably with the minimum of upsells.

Ease of Use

Your registrar, and their control panel, should be easy and intuitive to use. It should be easy to search for available domain names, and easy to buy them online.

Affordability

Domains offered should be affordable, and there should be no bar on their transfer or ability to point them at any given hosting you may possess.

Stability

You do not want to buy a domain name from a company that may not exist in two years' time.

Good Support

You want a registrar who provides a good level of support – preferably via online chat or by phone, at any time you need it.

There are many registrars out there, but two I recommend are:

http://1click123.com

http://alunrecommends.com/namecheap

5. Wrong Domain Name

It's easy to throw away all the benefits you have with the right hosting and registrar by selecting an inappropriate domain name.

Your domain name is what people are going to use to access your site. A little bit of thought before you buy one can save you a lot of heartache later on.

Domain Naming Tips

Use your name as your domain name, if it is available. E.g. I have alunrichards.com as the domain for one of my websites.

If you are intimately tied to the provision of your service and are somewhat known in your market, using your name as your domain, or part of your domain may be an option.

.com or, preferably .org .net

Always go for the .com variant if it's available, even if you have to add a word to the domain name, e.g.

onlinetrainingnow.com or
onlinetrainingtoday.com

If all the options have been exhausted, consider the .org or the .net variants. If you offer a lot of videos or webinars, consider the .tv option. Otherwise, ignore all the other extensions.

Use Your Keywords

What keywords are your target market using to find you as a provider of the service they want?

Use these keywords in your domain name.

If you have a popular niche, then you may find the most obvious keywords have been taken. However, with a bit of ingenuity, you should be able to find a keyword-rich domain that works for you.

Long Tail Keywords

Let's first distinguish short tail and long tail keywords. A short-tail keyword might be "weight loss". This will turn up a huge number of results in a search engine.

A long tail keyword string, or phrase, uses more search terms and is therefore more specific. An example might be "weight loss diabetic men over 45". This turns up far fewer search results, but those results are likely to be far more relevant to the person searching.

There are interesting differences in the use of these keywords. People who use short tail keywords are browsers are typically investigating the field. They are seeing what is available.

Users of long tail keywords on the other hand are typically buyers. They want to go straight to a solution that's right for their problem.

Buying a Domain With Long Tail Keywords

When you buy a domain with a long tail keyword phrase, you can be sure people searching for this will be close to wanting to buy. Also, as one of the main determinants of your position in Google is having your keywords in your domain name, you'll have an search engine advantage already.

Problem vs. Solution

People who say they are 'towards motivated' often have a problem with this, as they say it focuses on the negative rather than the positive.

But people who have a pressing problem will search for that specific problem as they want a resolution of it. They typically won't search for a type of solution, as they really don't care HOW the problem is solved, only that they get someone who understands their specific problem in depth and therefore has the resources to deal with it.

Many coaches and NLP practitioners find it hard to believe that there are so few searches for coaching, life coaching or NLP practitioner. One reason is that these are solution-oriented services whereas our customers will search for the pressing problem that they are experiencing.

So it's better to have the problem you solve in your keywords and in your domain name.

Another reason is that these terms are too general, and when people buy, they make their searches very specific.

Use Location, if Appropriate

More and more people are using the search engines rather than use "Yellow Pages" to find local businesses. If your business serves a local community, like a plumber, a locksmith, a restaurant or a decorator, then using your location in your domain name can help significantly.

A good domain name for a painter in La Jolla might be lajollahousepainter.com

This has search terms that might be searched for by people looking for a house painter, and a geographic area in which he operates - e.g. La Jolla.

A good UK example is Pimlico Plumbers - pimlicoplumbers.com.

Obviously if your service is countrywide or even global, this is not so relevant.

Benefits of a Good Domain Name

A good domain name should satisfy a number of criteria.

It should:

1. Be memorable by your target market.

2. Be search engine friendly - you get found easily by the search engines.

3. Not be in use already!

4. Describe what you do.

Problems With Domain Name

There are many problems to avoid when selecting a domain name.

Here are the main ones.

Different Spelling

You want to avoid picking a name that has a different spelling in the UK and US. Examples here are program/programme and color / colour.

Also, avoid picking a name that has different UK and US meanings. Examples are the words suspenders, pants and pavement.

Trying To Be Clever

Using numbers or letters as abbreviations:

e.g. solutions4u.com

The problem here is people won't know, on hearing it, if it's solutionsforyou.com, solutionsforu.com, solutions4you.com or solutions4u.com.

You should aim to select a domain name whose spelling is obvious when given over the phone.

Always aim for clarity, rather than being clever. If you don't, your target market could well end up at a competitor's website instead.

Domain Name That Can be Misinterpreted

Picking a long tail domain name that can easily be misunderstood when in a URL.

Here are a few domain names that had unintended meanings that perhaps the owner did not intend.

- therapistfinder.com

- whorepresents.com

- penisland.com

- powergenitalia.com

- expertsexchange.com

- molestationnursery.com

6. The Wrong Technology Choices

The problem with making the wrong technology choices is not that you can't create a website with them - if you have the skills and tools, you probably can. The problem is the on-going maintenance headache.

If you want a website that you can control yourself, you need a technology choice that is user-friendly, one that you can use yourself, if you choose to.

HTML Websites

HTML – HyperText Markup Language – is a language that was designed to build websites. Some years ago, you had limited choices as to how to build a website. The first websites were built in HTML, and you needed to understand HTML code to use it effectively.

Then visual editing tools like FrontPage and DreamWeaver emerged and they opened the door to more people creating websites. Instead of having to learn HTML, you could get by with a little HTML knowledge and the skills of using, say, FrontPage.

Many webmasters still use HTML because of the flexibility it gives you in layout. However, HTML has a number of disadvantages.

Needs Webmaster

Either you need webmaster skills, or you need to engage a webmaster to implement more than the most straightforward web page.

Maintenance Needs Programming Skills

When you need to edit anything in HTML, it's a multi-stage process. You need to first access a copy of the page you want to edit on your PC. Then you load it into (say) DreamWeaver, make your edits, and save it on your hard disk. Then you must transfer your edited page up to your hosting using ftp, carefully replacing the old page.

Expensive

As you need to go through this process even for changes to one sentence on a page, this process is very time-consuming. Because it takes webmasters a while to carry out such little changes, this ends up being expensive – typically £150 to change part of one sentence.

Flash Problems

Flash is a technology that makes really great looking sites. Flash is a display technology that allows you great control over images. Quite often, the whole front page of a site is a Flash image.

Expensive to Build

Flash sites can look ravishing, and it's perhaps why they are sought out by people offering high-end products and services.

One problem with Flash is that they have to be hand-created by a Flash programmer. And because of their complexity, this does not come cheap.

Design Skills and Marketing Skills Don't Often Coincide

The webmasters who have good design and Flash skills typically come from a graphic design background. This is great for layout and appearance. Unfortunately, to have an effective site that sells your products and services, you have to understand internet marketing. And Flash designers typically have a design rather than a marketing background.

So they are a great solution if you want a great looking website that doesn't effectively sell anything!

Expensive to Maintain

Because of the skill level required and cost of tools, Flash sites are very expensive to maintain. Unless you have good Flash skills already, you can discount this as a website option.

Doesn't Work on iPad and iPhone

With more internet traffic coming from smart phones, this is becoming an issue. Flash does not work at all on iPhones and iPads. A site built totally in Flash will show blank on an iPhone.

Site Builder Problems

I see people seduced by site builders all the time. Often they are a free option with many hosting platforms. And because they are free, people use them. While they are OK for your teenager's first website, so that Gran can see their creation online, they are not a solution for an online business.

"Oh but they're so easy to use" and "But it's free…" are the typical responses. There are a number of problems with site builders, and you'll find these problems to a lesser or greater extent depending on your choice of site builder.

Hard to Migrate

Once you have built a site with a site builder, you're stuck with it. The page layouts you've chosen won't be exportable to another site. There is no growth path. Site builders are a dead-end solution.

Limited Functionality

While at first it may seem easy to add images and change the page layout, once you want to add membership site functionality, add podcasting, secure product downloads, then you'll need to move to a more professional solution.

It's much better to start with a flexible, professional solution that you can grow with.

7. Poor Look & Feel

The most common problems in having a poor look and feel are due to a small number of root causes. It's sad because with the right tools, getting a good layout is easy – the tools do it for you.

Here the biggest look and feel mistakes.

Looks Homemade

I see this problem most often with site built with site builder software and with HTML sites that are created by people who don't really have the necessary HTML skills.

Poor Layout

You don't get a good-looking website just by posting a poor picture of you and cramming in a load of text with no thought about layout.

Good design is about balance of text against white space, balance of the various elements of the page and clean, functional design.

Poor Use of Fonts

What I see very often is many different fonts on the same page with many different colours. It looks like the children have been playing with as many crayons as they can get their hands on.

Have a look at the sites of established companies. They use a minimum of fonts and font sizes and they typically restrict their font colours to two.

Adverts from Site Builder

It's a mistake to use a free site builder especially if the adverts from the builder cannot be removed. Nothing labels you as an amateur more than advertising the tools you use rather than what you offer.

Website Not Functional

So many websites miss out on interaction with their visitors. They display details of the service they offer, but do it passively.

No Opt In Page

Marketers call a page that accepts your email address and your name a squeeze page. Not to have a squeeze page that builds your online prospect list is to squander the money you've spent on your website.

No Sales Page

You can't sell anything online unless you have a sales page. This page sets out what a prospective customer will get and has the ability to take payment and deliver the product or give details of how to get hold of the service you're providing.

Look upon a sales page as a salesperson in print. It represents you and your organisation, and outlines the benefits your prospect will gain from buying your offering.

You need to do one of three things to create your sales page.

1. Pay a copywriter to write copy for you.

2. Learn to write copy yourself.

3. Use a package that prompts you to write good copy.

No Contact Form

While it is perhaps understandable that some people don't have squeeze pages and sales pages, it defies logic why so many people don't even have a functional contact form on their site. This is like throwing business away – from prospects who have taken the trouble to visit your site.

No Prominent Phone Number

And if having no contact form were not bad enough, I see many websites that do not even have the owner's phone number prominently displayed. So many people bury their contact number so deep on an obscure page that prospects stand almost no chance of finding it.

Your phone number, assuming you want prospects to contact you, should be clear and preferably on your website banner.

About The Author

Alun Richards

Alun Richards has been setting up WordPress websites for small businesses for more than five years. In that time, he has helped countless clients to get their business online.

He worked as a senior management consultant for over twenty years, working with boards and senior managers from J. Sainsbury, the BBC, Ordnance Survey, BT and Esso.

Alun has an MBA from Cranfield School of Management, a Diploma in Marketing, an MSc in Information Systems Design and Management and a BSc in Physics from Imperial College.

In his easy-to-follow books, he guides you through setting up a WordPress website that will be your shop window on the world.

Alun is also the author of:

Fire Your Webmaster! Create Your Own WordPress Website And Save Yourself A Fortune.

Alun lives in Maida Vale with his wife Maricarmen and son Julian.

Success Stories

"I have been working with Alun Richards for 18 months, having first met him at conference when Alun was presenting.

Before I met Alun – I had no clue about all things internet, websites and it had never occurred to me that I could ever have products to offer my target market. Alun has helped me via his brilliant and precise teachings with his Internet Marketing Mentoring Programme, helping me to define my niche and work out what I can do and how I can best get information to my clients.

From having no web site and no clue, I now have a Word press website with autoresponder attached and video and am able to amend, adjust and enhance my own site – which is brilliant. I can at last refer people to a site that can grow alongside my business coaching business with pride.

Alun has given me so much knowledge and confidence to support my business. Recently I also invested in his Product Creation Teleclass – which has given me inspired ideas on which products will help my potential target market(s) and ways and means of getting this information to them in interesting formats.

Because of the way Alun structured his course, I always have the information to refer back to as teleseminars and webinars which are always available to review and very clear and concise downloadable workbooks which are brilliant reminders of what there is to learn.

In addition to learning from Alun, because I coach small business owners, I find that this knowledge is filtering through to my own clients, thus enhancing my own coaching practise with increased value to my clients which makes my coaching more unique.

I can highly recommend Alun's teleclasses, which are stuffed full of good and sound information and would not hesitate to recommend them to anyone. Absolutely brilliant! "

Karen MacFadyen

Moonstone Coaching Limited

"Alun has a wide range of knowledge about how to set up your own effective websites.

He explains technical concepts so that non-techies can understand and implement them.

I'd also tell other people (about his courses) that a good, knowledgeable bloke runs them and he's probably undercharging! I feel more confident about creating my own video PowerPoint presentations."

Phil Hampton

http://www.manageandlead.com/

"Alun provides great detail, is thorough and generous in giving useful information.

I now believe it is possible to have a website, which is going to generate income."

Jane Karsten

http://www.janekarsten.com/

"Alun actually cares about the value you get from his products and services and you can purchase in confidence that he is there to help and support you – not take your money and run!"

Nadine Honeybone

http://www.designsonlife.net/

"My recommendation to other people is to do a course with Alun! I already have recommended Alun's courses to two people specifically and praised them on Facebook.

I have gained a much deeper and broader understanding of how everything fits together. I have benefited from expert advice. I was able to ask those questions that were causing me to be stuck."

June Whittle

http://teacherskeepcalmandcarryon.com/